"Jim Breig has done an excellent job in drawing out the humanness of Jesus in this little gem of a book. I hope *The Emotional Jesus: How to Feel Good About Feelings* finds the wide readership it deserves."

Rev. Joseph Girzone
Author, *Joshua*

"*The Emotional Jesus* is a gem that will cause people to know Jesus differently. In it, Jim Breig makes Christ real. And by becoming aware of this emotional Jesus, readers will be allowed to name, own, and respect their own emotions. Scripture takes on new meaning, and Christians will become more real as they laugh, cry, love, and experience joy, just as Jesus did.

"This book offers practical ways to live our emotions fully. Through it, we come to know that Christians are to be emotional people."

Sr. Anne Bryan Smollin, C.S.J., Ph.D.
Author, *Jiggle Your Heart and Tickle Your Soul*

"I'm grateful that Jim Breig has focused on the issue of Jesus' emotions. Regretfully, most Christians, interested only in what the Lord said and accomplished, have ignored this essential component of his personality.

"This book nudges us back to the belief of the apostles and martyrs that, except for sin, Jesus truly became one of us. By spending even a little time learning more about the Lord's emotional personality, perhaps we'll be able to accept that aspect of our own personalities. I trust that Jim Breig's insights will provide an important first step for many into this rarely traveled realm."

Rev. Roger Karban
Belleville Diocese

"James Breig is a gifted writer with beautiful insights into the place of emotions in Christian spirituality. *The Emotional Jesus* is an enlightening, satisfying book, a wonderful reading experience that will open depths of everyday faith you may never have thought possible. Thank God such a book has finally been written."

Mitch Finley
Author, *The Gospel Truth: Living for Real in an Unreal World*

"Throughout his life Jesus demonstrated that human emotions are normal, natural, and neutral, part of being human. The author helps us to see the importance of expressing our emotions as Jesus did, who experienced frustration, exasperation, anger, disappointment and a whole range of emotional discomfort. This book will help you to draw closer to Jesus."

Rev. John Catoir
Director, The Christophers

"In compelling but simple language, James Breig presents the incarnate, flesh and blood Jesus as fully human, complete with emotions he did not suppress. This book is a halleluia for living the Christian life *with feeling*, and a welcome reminder that an unemotional Christian is a contradiction in terms."

Antoinette Bosco
Author, *The Pummeled Heart: Finding Peace Through Pain*

"Affectivity remains the underexplored and underdeveloped component of the Christian moral life and of Christian prayer. In *The Emotional Jesus*, James Breig focuses on the affective life of Jesus and shows how Jesus' deeply emotional life can inform our own. Perhaps one of the best recommendations for this book is that the reader is left wishing there were more of it!"

Pamela A. Smith, SS.C.M.
Author, *WomanStory: Biblical Models for Our Time*
and *WomanGifts: Biblical Models for Forming Church*

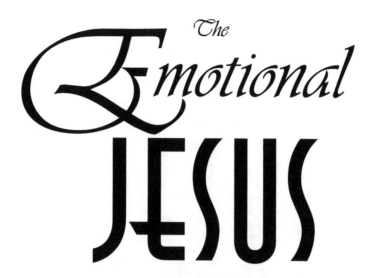

The Emotional JESUS

How to Feel Good
About Feelings

JAMES BREIG

TWENTY-THIRD PUBLICATIONS
Mystic, CT 06355

Twenty-Third Publications
185 Willow Street
P.O. Box 180
Mystic, CT 06355
(860) 536-2611
800-321-0411

ISBN 0-89622-669-7
Library of Congress Catalog Card Number 95-78542
Printed in the U.S.A.

Dedication

For Meaghan and Keegen,
and especially for 'P'

Contents

Introduction

Emotions
Are
Important

$\mathcal{T}$his book is for anyone God loves.

That means, of course, that this book is for everyone. More specifically, it's for anyone who loves God back or who feels the need to love God more. It's also for all of us who want to recognize, accept, and tap into the fact that our emotions are part of our human nature, and that without emotions, we are less than we should be, less than God intended us to be.

Some of us aren't even aware that without emotions, we are stunted and shrunken. Such people think of emotions—expressed in tears and smiles and embraces—as signs of weakness or as contradictions to intelligence. If that were so, then we would have to think of Jesus Christ as weak and ignorant. On the contrary, because he was a fully human being, he showed how to feel and express emotions in a fully human way.

This book is about the emotions Jesus felt when he walked around the Holy Land and it's about what he did with his emotions. It's also about what these emotions mean for us today. Jesus still loves us even as he sits at the right hand of the Father. Together with the Holy Spirit, Father and Son love us unconditionally. Love is partly intellectual and partly an act of the will. But love is also felt and expressed in emotions. Therefore, unless we tap into our emotions, we cannot fully respond to God's love or love ourselves or others.

As I explore the emotions of Christ in the following pages, I will, of course, refer to scripture. However, sprinkling citations from the Bible throughout a text sometimes turns reading, which should be a relaxed pastime, into a complex one. Sometimes in other books readers are asked to leap over brackets, vault parentheses, and dodge numerals in order to make sense out of sentences. But you won't have that trouble with this book. All of my scripture references appear at the back. There's an added bonus in

2

that: When you look up the citations, you'll find their context as well as related passages to read. You'll also find that I have freely paraphrased the Bible on occasion. If that stirs emotions in you, you're welcome.

Chapter One

Jesus
Got
Exasperated

Christians don't often think about it, but Jesus Christ had emotions. When they do think about it, Christians realize that Jesus was a human being, and all human beings have feelings. And like everything else about Jesus, his emotions are prefigured in the Hebrew Scriptures. An example is Ezra and his exasperation.

Ezra was a priest-scribe about 400 years before the birth of Christ, during the period that the Israelites were returning to their homeland from exile in Persia. He labored long and hard to restore the Jewish people to their homeland and to their traditions, and that meant separating them from the foreigners around them who too often had tempted them to move away from God.

In effect, Ezra said to the people, "If we just keep to ourselves, we'll be fine. Let the others go their way. Let us stay here, near the Temple in Jerusalem, and everyone will be happy."

One day he found out that many Israelites, including their leaders, had not separated themselves from the outsiders. On the contrary, they were cozying up to the Canaanites. And the Hittites. Oh, yes, and the Perizzites and the Jebusites. Also the Ammonites and Moabites. Ditto the Egyptians and the Amorites. In fact, lots of Israelite men were so universally cozy that they were marrying women from those nations and following their wives' pagan ways.

Ezra didn't take this news well. (Actually, that's an understatement.) Here's what Ezra did: "I tore my garment and my cloak; I tore hair from my head and beard, and sat down, quite overcome."

Overcome? Another translation says that he was "stupefied." He was so stupefied that he sat where he was—surrounded by tufts of hair and swatches of his clothes—for the remainder of the day, dumbfounded at how brainless his people could be.

Getting exasperated is a familiar refrain in the Old Testament. In fact, often it is Yahweh who is stupefied and dumbfounded. Even at the beginning, God said, "Have all the good things you want. Just don't touch the apples." But, of course, Adam and Eve picked the fruit and ate it, and got themselves—and us—tossed out of paradise.

That happened again and again throughout the Bible. "Tell the people not to worship other gods," Yahweh warned. But naturally, as soon as Moses was out of sight, the people crafted a golden calf and worshiped it.

"Let your hair grow, Samson, and you'll be stronger than anyone," God said. But Samson lingered around Delilah, who drugged him and, as soon as he was asleep, gleefully cut his hair.

"Be faithful, David," God warned. The poet-king, of course, convinced himself that lusting after Bathsheba and setting up her husband to be killed were the two minor exceptions to God's rules.

People in New Testament times exasperated God, too, and we continue to do so in our own lives today. "If you follow me, you will be saved," Jesus assures us. That's fine, we answer, but let us sin a while first.

God had good reason to be exasperated, and Jesus certainly did, too. As a human being, he presented a perfect example of what people are capable of. He showed us how to live, behave toward one another, think, and pray. But he not only breathed and walked and talked and prayed. He also *felt*. And by feeling, he taught us about emotions.

We can all cite examples of Jesus teaching us to pray, to give to others, to follow the Father's will. But most of us don't recall what Jesus taught us about emotions. By showing us that he had them, he was saying that emotions are normal, natural, and human—even exasperation!

An emotion, according to the *New Catholic Encyclopedia*, is a "felt tendency toward anything intuitively appraised as good, or away from anything intuitively appraised as bad. This attraction or aversion is accompanied by a pattern of physiological changes organized toward appropriate action."

In other words, something happens to us, and we react in a snap. We see someone beautiful, and we are attracted to him or her. Someone spits on us, and we get angry. A friend dies, and we feel sorrow. A rattlesnake crosses our path, and we jump in fright. Emotions usually come without warning and without our choosing them. Scientists don't agree about how emotions happen; they debate about chemical reactions and neurological synapses and evolutionary tendencies and learned behaviors. Whatever their origin, we know this about emotions: They are morally neutral because we do not will them to occur.

But we do choose what to do after our emotions arrive. And that choice brings us into the realm of morality, and back to Jesus. He not only showed us that emotions are normal and natural; he also showed us what he did with those emotions. How he experienced them, how he dealt with them, how he turned them into actions, and what that all means for us is what this book is about.

Consider Jesus' exasperation. It is one of his strongest emotions, resulting from the constant frustration and disappointment he encountered as he tried to teach people about his Father. A good example occurs in the Gospel of Mark. Right after raising a little girl from the dead, after walking on water, after multiplying the loaves and fishes, after restoring sound to a deaf man's ears, after curing "all those who touched Him," Jesus was approached by some Pharisees. Guess what they wanted. That's right, they wanted a sign from heaven.

"A what!" Jesus shouted. "Are you telling me the first dozen didn't count?"

Irritated, and probably through clenched teeth, Jesus told them to get lost. But before he did, he let out "a sigh that came straight from the heart." It was a sign of his heartfelt exasperation. The sort of sigh a harried mother might heave just before she heaves junior into his playpen after he scribbles with crayons all over the kitchen wall. The sort of sigh that says, "You're driving me nuts; you know that, don't you? Sometimes I think you do it on purpose."

But it wasn't only the annoyances of the inimical Pharisees that irritated Jesus. His closest friends could do it much better, and more often. Right after the Pharisees asked for signs, Jesus warned his followers to "watch out for the yeast of the Pharisees and the yeast of Herod."

Being the complete, literal-minded blockheads they were, the apostles whispered to one another: "He said that because we have no bread."

Overhearing them, Jesus—probably smacking his forehead good and hard—responded sharply: "What are you talking about? Are your minds closed? Don't you remember anything I've said so far?"

We can guess that they just stared blankly at him because he had to repeat his question: "Are you still without perception?" Then Jesus must have walked away shaking his head, slapping the sides of his legs, and muttering over and over, "Morons!"

Not too much later, a man asked the apostles to exorcise his son, but they bumbled the task. "How much longer must I put up with you?" Jesus asked, and he immediately proceeded to cast out the demon. When the apostles wondered why they botched the job, he said (I suspect with more than a touch of sarcasm), "Did it ever occur to you to try praying?"

Anyone who has ever tossed a bottle of pills across the

room after failing to work the child-proof cap can appreciate the exasperation Jesus felt one day when his stomach was rumbling with hunger. Spotting a fig tree and tasting the fruit's sweetness even before he got to it, he rushed to the tree, reached up for a fig and grabbed nothing but air. Royally annoyed at the barren limbs, he did what most of us would do: he cursed the tree. "Fine," he shouts. "If you're not going to have fruit on you now, then you never will." And it didn't.

Luke tells us another story about Jesus' exasperation. Thinking about John the Baptist, Jesus pondered how much his cousin was ignored and reviled by the people he prophesied to. "Let me think now," Jesus said, "How can I explain exactly how stupid you are? What are you like? Let me see...."

Then it came to him. Such people were like children horsing around and chanting: "We played the pipes for you, and you wouldn't dance. We sang dirges, and you wouldn't cry." In other words, a prophet came and told you about the coming Messiah and explained how to get right with God, and what did you do? You sat there, breathing through your mouths like dolts, and did nothing. Until it occurred to you to work up the energy to behead him.

Jesus' ultimate experience of exasperation, of course, occurred in the Garden of Gethsemane right before he was arrested. He asked his best friends to do one thing for him: "Keep awake." Of course, like Adam and David and Moses and Samson and us, they nodded—and then nodded off. Jesus returned to find them snoring away and repeated his one favor: "Just stay up for an hour, please." But tired and weak, they snoozed on and on.

It's good to know that Jesus got exasperated, because we get exasperated all the time, too. But there's a difference. We tend to get fed up over things that are of little importance, things like people not doing things our way...not clinging to our every word...not serving our needs first, last, and always. We get annoyed when a co-worker doesn't work as fast as we do and in the same order. We get riled because our children don't find our dinnertime homilies interesting. We even get aggravated when the U.S. Supreme Court or the Pope rules in a way we wouldn't have.

Sometimes we have legitimate reasons for being exasperated. When we've explained something four times in eight different ways and the listener still gets it wrong; when our teenagers ask, re-ask, and then ask again if they can stay out till 2 a.m.; when co-workers don't do their part and we have to work harder—those and many other circumstances call for exasperation.

However, a legitimate reason for exasperation doesn't mean that we should respond by hurting someone or cutting them off. Over and over, Jesus teaches us that what we choose to do after our feelings arrive involves morality. It is at that moment that we can opt to do right or to do wrong.

As Jesus shows by his own behavior, feelings just happen. After all, they are emotions, and the word "motion" is in there because they come fast, without planning, without our willing them. But once the emotion arrives, Jesus shows us, again by his own behavior, that we have to react intelligently and morally. The proper response to a feeling of exasperation is easy to discern by watching Jesus. He shows us how to take time to explain when there are people willing to learn and grow.

The answer to "How many times do I have to explain this to you?" is the same as the answer to "How many times do I have to forgive?" Seven times seventy, for starters. In short, whatever it takes.

Jesus was constantly explaining himself to those who would listen. No matter how many times he had to slap his forehead and wonder, "When are you going to figure this out?" he continued to teach: in parables, in aphorisms, by example, and even by carefully and slowly telling his apostles what each part of his stories meant. Sometimes they were very slow, not getting it at all. "The sower is the Son of Man," Jesus said to them. "Now do you get it?"

He explained and explained, and taught and taught, and repeated and repeated, always as patiently as he could. Notice that I didn't say he lectured and lectured, put down and put down. The follow-up to exasperation shouldn't be sarcasm or calling people names. It should be a resolution to change the explanation if it isn't understood, to listen to objections, to hear needs, and to give people time to absorb what's being said to them.

There is another proper response to exasperation that Jesus shows us: If you're up against a brick wall, walk away from it. Don't linger near something or someone that is making you crazy. The Pharisees were not open to listening to Jesus, so he refused to waste his time on them. When they caused so much stress in his life that it was even making his breathing difficult (a common sign of stress), he separated himself from them and joined his friends.

When we think about reacting to people who exasperate us, it might be helpful to think about the response we want when we exasperate someone else. Even Jesus knew about that. Remember his parents looking for him when he was twelve? After three days, they finally spied him in the temple. They were, the Gospel tells us, "overcome" and "worried." In other words, exasperated. They didn't understand his explanation, but they listened. His mom "stored up all these things in her heart," but I bet she still tapped her foot in irritation.

Chapter Two

Jesus
Felt
Pity

Again and again in the New Testament, the evangelists describe Jesus as being filled with pity. Some translations use the word "sorrow" instead. It's a poor substitute, but the translators chose it because the word "pity" has such negative connotations for modern readers.

But substituting "sorrow" for "pity" robs some of the richness from the stories about Jesus' feelings. Here's why: If you insert an "e" into pity, you get piety. And the connotation isn't just a Scrabble coincidence. The words "pity" and "piety" are related in their etymology. Unfortunately, they have something else in common: bad reputations. Today, both words connote weakness, which has limited their usage. Let's see if we can rehabilitate them by exploring how Jesus' pity connects to his piety. It's necessary work if we're going to understand why Jesus spent so much of his time pitying others.

"Pity" probably requires the most effort to recover. It's a pity that "pity" has such a negative image. Telling someone, "Your work is pitiful" is not likely to bring a smile of appreciation. "I pity you" is not heard as a soothing statement. "Pitiable conditions" slur the poor. "Such a pity" is a way of saying "What a waste."

Piety is only slightly less offensive. Remarking that someone is "pious" is just shy of calling that person a hypocrite. Pious people are pictured as self-righteous pray-it-alls who lord it over others.

But the dictionary can help take us back to the roots of those words. *Webster's Unabridged* defines pity as "sympathy with the grief or misery of another; compassion or fellow suffering." Even the first definition of "pitiful" is positive: "full of pity; tender; compassionate."

The word "pity," as already mentioned, has its etymology in "piety," which *Webster's* defines as "devotion to religious duties and practices." Jesus constantly reminded people that their religious duties involved more than ritual washing or not picking ears of corn on the Sabbath. He taught—and demonstrated by his actions—that piety leads to pity, and that both lead to right action on behalf of others.

To put it another way, Jesus' faith (his piety) led him to experience the emotion of pity quite frequently; and the way he dealt with that emotion was to try to change the pitiful situations he saw.

For example, Matthew tells us: "As Jesus stepped ashore, he saw a large crowd; and he took pity on them and healed their sick." There was always that three-part rhythm, the waltz of love in Jesus' life: he saw suffering people, felt compassion for them, and then did what he could to change the situation. He saw...took pity...and healed. That's a good formula for active Christianity as well as a strong antidote against those of us who like to perform that other three-step dance: to see...complain...and do nothing.

Time after time, Jesus felt pity—compassion, sympathy—for people. And time after time, he did something to relieve their problems, regardless of what they were.

When he encountered physical hunger, he told his apostles: "I feel pity for all these people; they have nothing to eat. I don't want to send them off without something. They might collapse from hunger." So he multiplied the loaves and fishes, and everyone in the crowd had plenty to eat.

Coming upon some people with physical handicaps, Jesus responded with just as much compassion. "There were two blind men sitting by the side of the road. Jesus felt pity for them and touched their eyes. And their sight returned."

Spiritual hunger constantly moved Jesus to do something. "He took pity on them because they were like sheep without a shepherd, and he set himself to teach them."

Seeing people beset with grief was another spur for his pity. "A dead man was being carried out for burial, the only son of his mother, a widow. When the Lord saw her, he felt pity for her. 'Do not cry,' he said. Then he raised the young man."

He fed people, he cured people, he taught people, he gave people life. He did so because he pitied them. And he pitied them because of his piety, that is, because of his eagerness to live out his relationship to his Father.

To put it another, more familiar way: Jesus practiced what he preached. Religion was not just a "be" thing to him. It was also a "do" thing. But it became a "do" thing only after it was a "feel" thing. After he was touched by what he saw, Jesus touched back and left the indelible impression of his existence.

Many modern Christians demonstrate this same one-two-three dance: to see, to pity, to help. They see something wrong, feel pity, and then set about to change what they see. Mother Teresa is one of the preeminent examples of this behavior, but there are millions of others like her who are not as famous.

A boy sees freezing homeless people, feels compassion for them, and takes them blankets, inspiring others to do the same.

A woman sees unwed mothers turning to abortion because they have no alternative, feels sorrow for them and their children, opens her home to them, and invents Birthright.

A black priest sees minority children abandoned by their parents, feels their loneliness, and adopts one. Others in the neighborhood say, "If he can do it, we can, too."

We all admire people like that. Most often though, we go only part of the way with Christ. We can see the problems of others, and we can feel compassion for those who are suffering. But too often that's where we stop. We don't do a *blessed* thing about what we see and how we feel (pun definitely intended). The horrible suffering of the starving poor, the terrible plight of war victims, the victims of destructive natural disasters, the soul-crushing poverty in our inner cities, the suicidal drug addictions of suburbia—we have witnessed them all. On our better days, we can feel the hunger, fear, hopelessness. But too often, we don't take the final steps with Jesus. We don't do anything. When we do take action, it is stunted. If we pray, we don't pray hard enough or long enough. If we give a donation, we don't give until it hurts. And we certainly don't reach out a hand and say, "Let me help."

It's a pity that our pity is so short-lived. If we have an excuse, it's because we all live in an age of problem overload and compassion fatigue. We can only watch so many dying children on television every night before turning the channel. How often can we send a check to a relief agency? How many letters to Congress can we pen? After a while, we begin to wear down and collapse under the weight of all the sorrow. One of the dangers of this overload is that we will stop feeling anything. Seeing so much and so many to pity, our emotions become scarred. When they stop prodding us, we stop doing anything, and the circumstances worsen.

When he sees us laid low, stymied by the world's pain, and filled with doubts about our responses (or lack thereof), I hope Jesus does what he has always done. I hope he feels pity for us and offers us solutions. Maybe he whispers: "You can't do it all, and you can't do it alone. But you can do something."

Even Jesus didn't cure every leper in the world. During his lifetime, he didn't feed the hungry in India or stop wars in Gaul or comfort earthquake victims in Japan. He did what he could and then asked his followers to carry on, extending his pity as far as humanly possible: to homeless people, unwed mothers, abandoned children, and to so many others in need.

Chapter Three

Jesus
Got
Angry

$\mathcal{I}$f there is one emotion that Jesus expressed that makes many of us uncomfortable and that makes him seem not so divine and far too human, it's anger.

Many people have trouble with Christ's temper, especially when he stomped into the temple, put together a makeshift whip as if he had been practicing for a long time, roared his disapproval, and started tossing out coins and doves and moneysellers at random.

Trying to squirm their way out of seeing their savior as an angry man, some Christians interpret the story allegorically. They say it's just a symbol of his new covenant overcoming the old one. Others hope that the story was added on by his followers to show their feelings rather than his. Any explanation is better than having to admit that Jesus was angry. For many Christians, conceding that their founder was furious would come close to saying that he sinned. Well, being angry *is* a sin, isn't it?

No. The emotion itself is not a sin. In fact, the opposite could be true. It could be a sin *not* to be angry when the occasion warrants it. To let some of life's injustices go by without getting furious demonstrates either ignorance, deliberate shortsightedness, or tolerance of evil, none of which is defensible. Anger at the absence of justice is not a failure. On the contrary, it can be the only proper response.

Rather than showing Jesus as less divine, his anger proves that he is totally human and experienced the range of feelings that human beings can have. And since he was also divine and could not sin, his rage proves that being angry is not a sin at all when it is properly felt and appropriately expressed.

What can be sinful is getting enraged over trifles or showing our anger in improper, unbalanced, or disproportionate ways. Jesus saved his ire for important matters, like the time he was in the synagogue in Capernaum and sensed that he was being set up. His accusers were hoping that he would cure a man's withered hand on the Sabbath, thus breaking the strictures against labor on the Lord's Day.

Jesus asked them a simple question: "Is it against the law to do good on the Sabbath?" No one answered; they would have had to agree with him that it obviously wasn't against the law. "Then grieved to find them so obstinate, he looked angrily around at them" and cured the man's hand.

"Take that!" you can almost hear him saying. Furious and indignant at their attempt to entrap him, he asked them to explain their position, was met with silence, and in effect waved two dismissive hands at them, his own and the cripple's.

The angriest Jesus is portrayed in the Gospel of Matthew, which contains several passages showing his outrage. And when Jesus got mad, he didn't attempt to bottle it up at all. It came out in sharp rebukes and harsh reproaches. Jesus advised his followers not to call their friend names; but when he got annoyed, he didn't hesitate to let off some steam with some well-chosen epithets. The classic instance is when he got mad at Peter and called him "Satan" for tempting him to put aside his mission.

Jesus got angry at things and places, too. He cursed the fruitless fig tree and hurled epithets at places like Chorizin and Bethsaida. Those were no mild remarks, either. They were full-blown condemnations for failing to heed his words. Working up a head of wrathful steam at Capernaum, Jesus says, "You think you're so hot? You think your citizens are going to heaven? Just the opposite! If the miracles I did in you had been done in Sodom, the folks there would have believed, and it wouldn't have been blown off the face of the earth. You're far worse than that hell-hole."

One of the main targets of Christ's wrath was two-faced religious leaders who didn't follow their own rules. When he got going on them, he had many choice phrases: brood of vipers, blind guides, fools, whitewashed tombs full of dead bones and corruption, serpents. In that same peroration, Jesus uses the word "hypocrites" seven times, just in case they missed his point the first or third or fifth time around.

The modern term for what Jesus did is "venting," and he did a lot of it. He didn't let himself get pushed around; he didn't shut up for fear of what others would say about him; he didn't dilute his message when it proved distasteful for some; he certainly didn't say, "Well, everyone's entitled to his or her opinion."

When he saw injustice, he let people know about it. But this is important to remember: In letting his rage out, Jesus never directed it at the wrong person, and he never did anything violent against people. When Peter contradicted him, Jesus nailed him, not the other apostles. When the Pharisees made him angry, he laid into them, not their followers. On the occasion when he got the most physically riled up, he stormed into the temple and overturned tables and chairs. He did not punch anyone in the nose.

We have trouble with an angry Jesus because anger seems to negate his love, mercy, and compassion. But legitimate anger and real love are not necessarily opposites. In fact, they often exist side-by-side. When a husband becomes angry at his alcoholic wife for neglecting their children and yells, "You have to get help," his love for her and them is being shown. A mother who gets mad at her toddler for wandering into the street yells at him out of affection and concern. Parents who see a report card dotted with "D's" and growl their irritation are expressing love for their child.

The inappropriate expression of anger, physical violence, for example, or the silent treatment, is what gives anger a bad name. But the bad name should be pinned on the expression of anger, not on the emotion itself. Anger is good when it arises from a suitable cause, when it releases tension, when it is properly directed, when it is expressed correctly, and when it is followed by actions designed to rectify its cause: when the husband takes his wife to an alcohol counselor, when the mother instructs her toddler about traffic safety, when parents meet with their child's teacher or hire a tutor.

Anger has to be expressed and let go. Otherwise, it will eat into people like rust. A friend who is a therapist puts it this way: "There are virtually no benefits in holding onto anger. Some people tell every available ear the story over and over and over again. The only thing that does is rehearse the anger. There is no therapeutic value in it. It does not release the anger. It only builds a larger pot of anger and creates more of a case for one to be angry."

We think of anger as sinful because we make it so. We get ticked off at stupid things ("The damn cable TV is off again"). When we get angry at things that deserve our rage, we often misdirect it, blaming the wrong people or telling others to fix what we should deal with ourselves. We show our ire in misguided ways ("That'll teach you to lie; do you want another swat?"). We hang on to anger as if it were a winning lottery ticket, walking around with sour faces, grumbling and moaning. We can even turn our anger back on ourselves, seeing ourselves as worthless.

I'm capable of all those things. A major league shortstop who boots a two-hopper is the recipient of curses from me, and he can't hear me. In fact, he's not even in the same city as I am. Annoyed with the credit card company, I tell my wife, "Just call and give them a piece of your mind..." as if it were her problem. I am capable of harboring anger for several days, allowing it to carve a bleeding ulcer here and weaken a major artery there.

Jesus did none of those things. When he felt anger, he expressed it, and then let it go. He set about trying to correct the situations that enraged him. When he was frustrated in that effort, he got mad again, let people know it, and then went on trying to change the circumstances for the better. Sometimes he walked away if he thought it was a lost cause or not worth additional emotion.

Those are not the actions of someone who is not human; those are not the actions of someone who is a sinner. Rather, those are the actions of someone living a healthy and fully human life. They are actions we need to learn and imitate in order to make proper use of anger in our own lives.

Chapter Four

Jesus
Felt
Fear

We're afraid of fear. We're taught from infancy to hide our fright and to be brave. "Don't be afraid" is among the first pieces of advice given to children as they learn to walk, or pet the neighbor's rottweiler, or go to school, or use scissors, or get a vaccination. When we say, "Don't be afraid," very often we mean, "Deny your feelings" or "You're weak if you feel fear."

Too many of us have been instructed to show a brave face, to go into battle like a hero, to grin and bear it, to take it like a grown-up. We are even told to bear the pain of childbirth or divorce or abuse with resignation. People who are afraid are ridiculed as fraidy-cats, yellow bellies, lily-livers, cowards, and wimps.

The emotion of fear, we soon learn from such lessons, is a sign of weakness. "Never let them see you sweat" is one way of expressing our fear of fear and our identification of fright as a defect of character. But this is advice that Jesus ignored. He even let people see him sweat blood. That's because he knew that being afraid was completely normal.

By expressing his fear, Jesus teaches us that it is not a flaw. Rather, it is a completely natural reaction to something frightening. Fear can save us. When we pull back in fear as a punch heads in our direction, we're likely to avoid a broken nose. When we flee from places where muggings occur, we probably avoid being robbed, or worse. Like other emotions, fear is normal; it is not wrong to be afraid. But it can be wrong to let fear dominate our lives and paralyze us. It can be wrong to let fear develop into excessive worry or despair.

Jesus knew how to handle fear. He used a five-step process: Let it out, face it, replace it with courage, put matters in God's hands, and then act.

Step 1: Let it out. Jesus experienced his worst case of fear during his agony in Gethsemane. The reason is obvious: He was facing the most frightening thing in life, imminent death. He knew he didn't have long to live if he stayed where he was. So he shook with fright and was "in great distress."

Step 2: Face it. There is one sure way to double our fear: deny it exists. Fear is like rust or a rash—the more it is ignored, the more it increases. Once it is dealt with, on the other hand, fear begins to diminish. One way to face fright is to share it with someone else who can listen, understand, and sympathize. In Gethsemane, Jesus did that with his Father, even trying to bargain his way out of the crucifixion.

Step 3: Replace it with courage. Turned over like a coin, fear will show its other surprising face: courage. When others grew frightened, Jesus told them to calm down, have faith, and be brave. "Why are you afraid?" he would ask, inviting them to identify their fear and face it. That's what happened, for example, in the boat where he slept while the apostles got worked up over a storm.

Step 4: Put matters in God's hands. Faith that God has our best interest in mind should calm our fears. "Do not be afraid. Only have faith," Jesus tells Jairus when the official trembles over his child's death. It is advice Jesus follows himself as he shudders in the garden the night of his arrest. "Your will be done," he repeats over and over, finding courage in his faith in his father.

Step 5: Act. To sit and worry accomplishes little. Knowing what we are afraid of and confronting it puts us in charge. When we do that, to paraphrase Franklin Roosevelt, we may be defeated by what we fear, but we will not be defeated by the fear itself. Trembling in the garden, anguished about his impending death, Jesus does not run away and hide. Instead, he stands up and faces his accusers.

Heroes are not people without fear. They are people who

act in spite of their fear, who learn to manage their fear, who identify the cause of it and confront it. When Shakespeare said that the coward dies a thousand times while a brave person dies but once, he recognized the little, daily deaths that kill people who allow their fears to run their lives.

For most people, it is not dramatic things like arrest and execution that terrify them. It is the scary events of everyday life: making a speech, going to the doctor, asking for a raise, confronting a child's unfair teacher, picketing city hall, contradicting a superior.

Sometimes we're not even sure what we fear, and we tremble at our unnamed fear, unable to explain precisely what scares us. Since it has no name, we can't confront it, and it grows stronger. We hide from it, avoiding situations that frighten us, which usually makes those situations even worse and more frightening. We never think of asking for God's guidance or comfort. And the last thing we usually do is to face the fear head on. As a result, fear wins another round, nothing good gets done, and we become even less able to function.

Imagine Jesus making such choices. Full of agony in the garden, he might have said, "I'm afraid, but I'm not sure why. I'll feel better if I think of something else. I'm sure of one thing: It's a good idea to get out of here and put danger in the distance. Nazareth, here I come!" In such a scenario, Jesus would have denied his mission and put off the inevitable for just a little longer. He didn't do that, however. He accepted what was happening and experienced fear.

Following the example of Christ, we can name our fears, find ways to deal with them, and put our feelings in God's hands. We can also do something to change the cause of our fear. All of this means taking risks. Telling the drug dealer to get off the street corner could get us shot; letting the boss know what we think could get us fired; expressing an opinion on a social issue could get us ostracized in our neighborhoods. But all of those are preferable to living with fear.

Jesus shows us that it's completely natural and human to be afraid. He also shows us that the best human response to fear is courage, the sort of courage that might not dispel fear but that will deal with it. It is the sort of courage that exists despite fear, not because fear is absent. Finding courage requires an act of will because our automatic response to fear is to head for the hills. But by facing our fear, we can avoid what comes when fear festers: worry.

Worry gnaws at our stomachs and psyches; it chews on our minds and souls; it raises our blood pressure and lowers our self-esteem. Jesus knew fear, but he never worried. That's because he knew that his father was with him. Trying to give his followers the same sense of security, he promised two things: that they would eventually be with him forever, and that he would send his Spirit to stay with them until he returned.

There are fearful things in the world and in our lives, but that doesn't mean we have to fret over them, allowing anxiety to take control of our minds and hearts. Some of us are so addicted to worry that we even worry about things that haven't happened yet and might never occur at all. What if I get cancer? What will I do if I lose my job? How would I react if I were mugged? Where would I go if my house burned down? We plague ourselves with so many worries that there isn't room inside us for anything positive.

Jesus permitted himself only a short time in the garden to worry about what he faced. Then he said, "Your will be done" and went on with what remained of his life.

The next time you're afraid, remember what Jesus told us

about fear and worry: "What are you fretting about? Doesn't God love you? God takes care of the birds and squirrels and spiders and bacteria, and knows every time a paramecium twitches its tail. Don't you think God loves you about a zillion times as much? And don't fret over tomorrow or what might happen. Today has enough troubles. What is worry going to get you anyway? It certainly won't lengthen your life. It might even shorten it. God is on your side. People who worry have weak faith. They don't trust that God is with them. Don't worry; God is."

Chapter Five

Jesus Loved
and
Was Lovable

It's a cliché to talk about Jesus' love. It's the one emotion we're positive he had. Everyone knows that he felt love, showed love, and wanted us to do the same.

But what sort of love did Jesus experience and express? Too often, we imagine some sort of amorphous, gauzy love, an idealized love, a disembodied love, a vague idea of love. We say that God is love, but what do we mean? We say that Jesus loves us without limit, but what does that mean?

Those are questions we have to answer because when Jesus was asked to name the greatest commandment, he chose love in three directions: up, out, and inward. The three directions described love of God, love of neighbor, and love of self. He also told us how we should love: with all our heart, with all our soul, and with all our mind, physically, spiritually, and intellectually. Inward, unstintingly, totally, and forever.

As always, Jesus didn't just tell us about the feeling of love. Through his example, he showed us how to love. Jesus is love-able. Break the word apart, and it has two meanings: 1. Jesus is able to be loved; 2. Jesus is able to love. And he did both in several different ways. His love was neither ethereal nor undefined. It was a love that followed his definition of perfect love. It was a love that touched—acted physically—expressing all his heart. It was a love that cried—acted spiritually—displaying all his soul; and it was a love that spoke—operating intellectually—offering all his mind. Let's look at these one at a time.

1. The Touching Love of Jesus

When Jesus felt love, he loved to feel. His most touching occasions were just that, occasions when he touched. There is hardly a page in the Gospels where Jesus is not touching someone. He had a body, and he used it to express his feelings. He brings a precious little child close to him and drapes his arms around her while making a point to his followers. When parents bring their children to see him, he "puts his arms around them, lays his hands on them, and gives them his blessing."

When Jesus heals, he touches people. These phrases appear in the Gospel of Mark alone: "He went to her, took her by the hand and helped her up... Jesus stretched out his hand and touched him... taking the child by the hand, he said to her: 'Little girl, get up'... all those who touched him were cured... He put his fingers into the man's ears and touched his tongue with spittle... They brought him a blind man whom they begged him to touch. He put spittle on the man's eyes and placed his hands on him, and the man saw clearly."

The Last Supper and Jesus' final days abound with touching scenes, figuratively and literally. Jesus puts a towel around his waist, gets down on his hands and knees, and washes his disciples' feet. An unnamed apostle (probably John) leans his head on Christ's chest. At this dinner, he leaves his followers the Eucharist, an everlasting way to stay in touch with him, physically and spiritually.

2. The Tears of Jesus

"Jesus wept" is the shortest verse in the Bible, but one of the most meaningful, because it confirms for us how really human Jesus was.

Twice the Gospels record that Jesus cried, both times from sorrow and grief, because his soul was in great turmoil. One occasion was when a close friend, Lazarus, died. But here's the unusual part: Jesus knew that he was going to raise his friend from the grave. Nevertheless, he cried—in solidarity with his other friends and because Lazarus had been suffering. That's like what we do today when we weep over dead loved ones, even though we believe they are happy in heaven. That knowledge may put our grief in a spiritual context, but it certainly doesn't cancel it. That's why Jesus joins Lazarus's sister and other friends in weeping over him.

"At the sight of her tears and those of the Jews who followed her," John's Gospel reports, "Jesus was in great distress, and a sigh came straight from his heart. Jesus wept, and the Jews said, 'See how much he loved Lazarus.'"

The other time Jesus cried was over Jerusalem, representing not only itself but the entire Chosen People. Looking over the city, "he shed tears over it" because he knew it would be destroyed.

3. A Love Letter from Jesus

Jesus has written us a love letter. If we want to read it, all we have to do is open a Bible to chapters 12 through 17 in John's Gospel. In a series of prayers, parables, and promises, Jesus tells us exactly how much he loves us and invites us to love him just as much.

In those chapters, he outlines everything we need to know about his loving feelings: he will die for us; he will redeem us; he will stay with us; he will serve us; he will keep a place in heaven for us; he will pray for us; he will send us his spirit; he will make his home in us; he will comfort us; he will be part of us; he will come back to us.

He will, in short, love us as his Father loved him. His message can be summarized in just a few words, but it is extensive in its challenge: "Love one another as I have loved you."

Love one another with all our hearts, souls, and minds. Love one another by touching, and connecting, and giving, not by exploiting, or using, or taking. Love one another by weeping with, and being compassionate toward, and sacrificing, not by scorning, or ridiculing, or devouring. Love one another by writing love letters, singing, and saying, "I love you," not by ignoring, becoming cold, or growing neglectful. Love one another by sharing, not by condemning, or ignoring, or being selfish.

Although it might seem impossible to do, it's within our ability to love as Jesus did. To prove it, he left a blueprint for doing so in his Sermon on the Mount: By being poor in spirit, by being gentle, by being compassionate, by being seekers of justice, by being merciful, by being pure in spirit, by being peacemakers, by suffering on behalf of what's right, we can love as he loves.

It can be done, and Jesus shows us how.

Chapter Six

Jesus
Was
Sentimental

It would be nice if Scripture told us just once that "Jesus laughed." We know he cried, but the evangelists don't tell us that he slapped his thigh and guffawed. We have to read between the lines to find his sense of humor: in the pun about Peter's name, in the parables that use the familiar joke-teller's device of switched expectations, in the references to the camaraderie he enjoyed, in the scenes of relaxation around dinner tables, and in the references to his joy.

Jesus shared his joy so completely with others that "joy" is one of the last words in the Gospel of Luke. We know he wanted to share his joy, because he told his apostles earlier: "If you follow my words, my joy will be in you, and your joy will be complete." He then explained that total joy awaits them after the sorrow of this world.

The happy Jesus has to be searched for because his happiness was subtle, quiet, low-key. It can be seen in the delicate, tender feelings he often showed. He could be sentimental about people and places, a feeling that expressed his happy side and shows us what he enjoyed the most.

The word "sentimental" can be troublesome if it is heard as "sentimentality," the cloying and maudlin imitation of feeling that has no depth. To be honestly sentimental means to be genuinely moved, especially by the ordinary things of life that occur and reoccur every day—things like friends, hometowns, pets, alma maters, photographs, souvenirs, old teddy bears, and tree houses.

Jesus held his favorite things in his heart and sometimes called them to mind almost as salves against the worst sorrows and pains he had to face. From the cross, for example, he could see two of his favorite people: his mother and John, the disciple he loved. As he began to fade from life, he gave one to the other, uniting them for life.

As already cited, Lazarus was another close friend to whom Jesus had a sentimental attachment. Lazarus was "the man he loved" so much that he raised him from the grave. (In Hebrew, by the way, Lazarus means "God helps"; being brought back from the tomb is a nice bit of divine assistance.)

Scripture scholars have remarked that Jesus' parables don't contain proper names. He talked about "a farmer" and "a woman" and "a certain judge." The scholars wonder why Jesus broke that habit and named the poor man in his story about the beggar and the wealthy man. I suspect it's a case of sentimental Jesus winking his eye and teasing his back-from-the-tomb friend by using the name Lazarus for the wretch covered with sores.

Jesus' sentimental attachment to his disciples shows up all through the Gospels. Seeing them so busy that they didn't have time for themselves or even a second to grab a sandwich, Jesus said to them, "Let's get out of here; you guys need a break." At his last Passover, Jesus longed to dine with them and told Peter, "I pray for you all the time." He showed this feeling powerfully by donning an apron, getting down on his knees, and scrubbing his friends' feet. These were the friends he didn't want to leave, saying to them at the end of Matthew's Gospel: "I am with you always, even to the end of time."

Jesus also had sentimental feelings for Jerusalem, the city where he was taken as a baby to be circumcised, the place he went with his parents to celebrate and pray, the site where he preached and taught, the location of his death and resurrection. Talking about the city he cried over, he uses his most sentimental description of his own feelings, saying: "How I long to gather your children as a hen gathers her brood under her wings." That's a wonderful image of protective, loving, and self-sacrificing sentiment.

Jesus was often sentimental in describing how he and his

Father feel about human beings. To demonstrate his tender love for people, he talked about shepherds and lost sheep, old women and lost coins, lamps and farmers, and many types of household items, including yeast, bread, and salt. Those images bring God as close to us as our dinner table. They are everyday, mundane, common images.

They are, in a word, sentimental images. They show Jesus as an ordinary man interested in ordinary things. They also show Jesus telling us that God's love and our love in return should be as natural to us as table salt, as common as breakfast cereal, and as bountiful as daisies.

We live our love in the workaday world. We may sing songs about flying to the moon or diving into the sea for our beloved, but we are far more likely to show our affection by driving to work every morning and paying the bills every month. It's in the nitty-gritty details of daily life that we show our deepest love for others.

The sentimental Jesus showed his friends that he loved them by splitting his fish and bread with them, by relaxing with them in a rocking rowboat, by swapping stories, and by taking long walks with them. Then, like a relative who could not bear to part with his family, he left them himself in bread and wine, and sent his Spirit so that they would never be separated.

Chapter Seven

Jesus
Felt
Passion

When we think of Jesus' last hours, we picture the dramatic scenes so often portrayed in paintings and movies: the quiet gathering at the Last Supper; the twilight tension in the Garden of Gethsemane; the treacherous injustice of the trials; the lashing horror of the scourging; the lingering pain along the Via Dolorosa; and the lightning-lit Mount of Golgotha.

We call this time his Passion. The word means "suffering," but it also means "compelling emotion" and "intense emotional drive." That's what we mean when we talk about someone's passion for music or a passionate love affair. It should also be part of what we mean when we talk about Jesus Christ's Passion.

During his Passion, Jesus experienced and expressed a wide range of feelings, compressing the emotions he had shown over three years into a few hours, reaffirming once more that he was a real-life human being.

The exasperation that he so often expressed in sighs was present as he stood in trial before Pilate and the Pharisees. They were not interested in his defense or in the truth. Anyone who knows Jesus' response to the exasperation he felt years earlier when confronted by people with closed minds should not be surprised that he refused to answer their questions.

"Jesus was silent," Matthew tells us. Of course he was. It is the same silence he offered to others who would not listen to him during his ministry. "Let those with ears hear," he was fond of saying. He never wasted his time or breath on those whose ears were clogged and who had no interest in his words. To have wasted time on those people would only have exasperated him more.

Even after he rose from the dead, Jesus still got exasperated with his followers, indicating not only that emotions are normal but also that they continue after death. On the road to Emmaus, he said to two of his disciples, "You're still such dummies! You were told that the Messiah would suffer and die, and so it happened. Yet you are still shocked. What will it take to get through to you?" Later, appearing to the Apostles, he "reproached them for their incredulity and obstinacy" and told them to get out of their hiding place and get to work spreading the Good News.

Muted but not gone in these final scenes is Jesus' anger. In Gethsemane, he was sarcastic toward those who came to arrest him, asking, "What took you so long? I used to be next door to you, and you didn't lift a finger. Now you come all the way out here to get me. What am I? A pirate?"

After Peter struck Malchus with a sword, cutting off his ear, Jesus firmly rejected the sinful violence against others that anger so often engenders. Later, when Peter denied him, Jesus did not openly criticize his friend. He did, however, turn and look straight at Peter. We can only imagine how Peter felt at that moment.

Jesus' pity didn't desert him then either. Hanging on the cross and about to die, he showed compassion for those who crucified him and for one of the thieves hanging beside him. He asked his father's forgiveness on the soldiers who pounded the nails into him, and he promised paradise to the criminal who asked for mercy.

We have already covered the fear that Jesus felt during his final hours. And there should be no need to talk about his love during those closing moments. It was the preeminent emotion he expressed throughout his life; a centrality that did not change as he hung from a cross. It was for this act of redeeming love that he came into the world.

The Gospel of John comes to a close with the risen Lord on the shores of the Sea of Galilee with his apostles. They cook fish over a fire together, once again showing how love is lived out in ordinary moments. After they finish their breakfast and lean back on their elbows against the sand, Jesus has a question for Peter: "Do you love me?"

He asks it three times, echoing the three denials of Peter, uttered only days before. Scripture scholars tell us that in the original text, John uses different versions of the word "love" so that Jesus' question is inclusive of both the love between friends and the love that extends to all people (what we call charity). Also significant is that Jesus chose this emotion as his final message—and legacy—to his followers and to us.

Chapter Eight

Jesus Had
Emotional
Followers

So far, we have said that because Jesus was a human being, he had emotions. Those emotions often motivated his actions. Because Jesus is also the incarnate Son of God, he was like us in all things but sin. Therefore, he expressed his emotions in perfect and exemplary ways.

His earliest followers wanted to imitate him in every way they could. Therefore, they tried to express their own emotions similarly. That meant trying to use their emotions and not letting their emotions use them. But because they were human and imperfect, they did not always succeed. That truth applies not only to Christ's apostles, but to the saints throughout the ages and to us.

Jesus handled his emotions perfectly. To see how badly a human being can be misguided by emotions, we don't have to look any farther than the man who so often stood right beside Jesus: Peter.

Peter was obviously emotional and he had great difficulty controlling himself. In the Gospels he comes across as a man ruled by his emotions. And there is also hardly a moment when he does not get in trouble as a result.

His original name, Simon (or Simeon), means "God has heard." I would add the suitable phrase "an earful." Simon Peter liked to shoot off his mouth and act on his emotions without passing them through his brain first.

Jesus nicknamed Simon "the rock" (Peter), maybe because he was so steady, but also maybe because he was so hard-headed. When Jesus was afraid, he recognized it and confronted it. When Peter was afraid, which was often, he sank like the stone he was named after—literally. Seeing Jesus walk on water, Peter got very emotional. He was frightened at first, but then felt emboldened to step out on the water, trying his own big feet at water-walking. Called by the Lord, Peter didn't think twice. He leapt from the boat, but almost immediately he again felt frightened and doubtful, and he started to sink.

That's a common pattern for Peter in the Gospels. He reacts rashly and emotionally, never stopping to think or consider what might happen as a result of his actions, and he often ends up in tears. The classic scene, of course, occurs when Peter denied his best friend three times. Peter was told by Jesus, whom he had come to believe was the Messiah, that he would deny him three times. Having Jesus tell us what's going to happen is pretty good proof it will, but Peter didn't take time to consider the source. Offended and cocky, he blurted out, "Not me, Lord. These others might fold, but not the Rock. I'd go to prison or die first."

Within a few hours, Peter had fulfilled Jesus' prophecy. Filled with fear, he swore up and down and over again that he had never even laid eyes on Jesus, much less hung around with him every day for three years. When his emotional response faded, Peter realized what he had done and he wept bitterly.

Peter's fear was not his only emotion, or the only example of how he mishandled his feelings. His passionate response to anger contrasted sharply with Jesus' in the Garden of Gethsemane. Upset at his friend's arrest, Peter didn't pause even a second to contemplate what was happening. He whipped out his sword and sliced off Malchus's ear. Jesus had to rebuke him, and that was not the first time their relationship had involved Peter's rashly emotional behavior followed by reproach. Indeed, reproach might be too light a word to describe what happened the day Jesus called him, "You Satan," for trying to tempt him from his mission.

In many ways, the Peter of the Gospels is like a child. He almost always reacted quickly and emotionally, responding to stimuli the way a newborn baby does: Poke it, it cries; feed it, it coos; rock it, it falls asleep. Indeed, perhaps Peter was called "Rock" because he was so prone to falling off to sleep—in the boat, at the Transfiguration, in Gethsemane. At the Transfiguration, he also wanted to pitch a tent and stay on the mountain, an idea so childish that Luke says, "He didn't know what he was talking about."

When he gave up everything for Jesus, Peter wanted to know—like a greedy teenager—"What's in it for me?" Like a petulant adolescent, he refused to let Jesus wash his feet. When Jesus said that Peter must let him or they weren't friends, Peter responded with typically operatic emotionalism: "Then wash my legs and chest and arms and head, and wash my hair, too, while you're at it."

But it was this impetuous apostle who became the leader among Jesus' followers. Peter slowly learned to temper his temper—and his other emotions. When Jesus appeared to the disciples at the Sea of Galilee, Peter again jumped in the water. This time, however, he made sure he was not in over his head. When Jesus asked him a third time if he loved him, Peter got upset, not angry. When Jesus told him about the destiny he faced and what fate John faced, Peter became confused, but not resentful.

The adult Peter has now taken form, a form that will exert itself less emotionally and more intellectually, as evidenced in the Acts of the Apostles and the Epistles. In Acts, Luke tells us that Peter spoke for a long time and used many arguments to win converts. The brain had become Peter's sword. He didn't cut off ears; he filled them with the Good News.

Full of the Spirit himself, Peter still had emotions; but they were mature ones, and they were dealt with maturely. The fear and anger diminished to be replaced by courage and joy. When he was persecuted, Peter did not deny his Lord, and he did not flee. The Apostle who was so greedy that he wanted to know his particular reward became the man who invited all races to share in Jesus' kingdom.

As he wrote his first letter, Peter must have thought about his own behavior in the garden and in the courtyard when he denied Jesus. Then he cautioned others "never to pay back one wrong with another, or an angry word with another one. There is no need to be afraid or worried. Keep a calm mind."

Keep a calm mind! What wonderful advice from someone who had learned the hard way. He was hardly calm during those first three years of following Jesus. Eventually he gained control of his emotions, and he found in them a way to honor his Messiah: joyfully, courageously, and inclusively.

I suspect that Peter began to learn emotional control as he sat on the beach with the risen Christ. Jesus asked three times if Peter loved him. Each time that Peter said yes, Jesus told him to do something: Feed my lambs...look after my sheep...feed my sheep. This was the patient, loving Jesus explaining one last time that emotions (like love) must lead to good actions.

Peter proved to be a studious pupil. So did the other apostles. So did the followers of Christ we now call saints, both those canonized and those who are unsung. Through the centuries, their emotions became spurs to positive action. Consider these heroes and heroines:

Vincent de Paul's anger at the treatment of galley slaves led him to open homes for the poor, to establish hospitals and orphanages, and to ransom slaves.

Elizabeth Seton's love for poor children, especially girls who were left uneducated, led her to become the foundress of a nationwide Catholic school system.

Joseph de Veuster, whose religious name was Father Damien, felt pity for lepers and this led him to minister to them even after he had contracted the disease himself. His legacy includes treatment centers, schools, and libraries.

Martin de Porres's love for the poor resulted in the creation of orphanages, foundling hospitals, charitable institutions, and housing for the needy.

Elizabeth of Portugal, a royal woman, felt so deeply about the poor that she opened her palace to them, paid the dowries of impoverished girls, and set up hospitals and refuges for the neglected.

When Jesus was asked to explain who our neighbors are, he told the parable of the Good Samaritan. It is a story filled with emotions: the terror of the victim, the fear felt by the priest and Levite, the pity of the Samaritan. It is the compassionate Samaritan who does something about the man in pain. Jesus' instruction to us is simple: "Go and do the same yourself."

Chapter Nine

Emotions
and
Christians Today

$\mathcal{F}$ounded by and named after an emotional man, Christianity should be a religion of emotional people. For centuries and throughout the world, it has been that for many followers of Jesus. Christian individuals and groups have displayed their emotions without shame.

St. Paul's enthusiasm is contagious in his letters. Francis of Assisi loved all of creation and sang songs of praise and joy. Teresa of Avila was ardent in her faith, the "Little Flower" felt the pain of little things with joy, John XXIII was exuberant and loving, Martin Luther King overcame fear to denounce racism, and Mother Teresa's pity, etched on her cheeks and forehead, is obvious to all.

Shakers shake with emotion in England. Charismatics ululate with bliss in Germany. Holy rollers dance with ecstasy in Georgia. Fundamentalist preachers pound the pulpit in exasperation in Australia. Hispanics sing, Native Americans chant, Italians parade, and black Catholics shout "Amen." All declare their faith with great emotion.

But there are also millions of silent, still, stone-faced, almost emotionless Christians. They feel at least fear: fear of emotion. To them, emotions are dangerous things at best; sinful things at worst. They have been taught to be quiet, follow instructions, and "think" their way into heaven.

Prayer is not an emotional experience for such Christians; it is an intellectual exercise. Worship is not a time to sing and smile, but to sit, stand, and kneel glumly. Such Christians resent and resist moments that invite them to be emotional; they don't want lively hymns or handshakes of peace. They mutter the Great Amen instead of shouting it. They shrug when invited to share the Good News. When they receive the body and blood of Christ, their "Amens" sound like "Yeah, right."

These same Christians are no doubt capable of showing

emotions on other occasions: At the ballpark, at company picnics, meeting new co-workers, enjoying good food. Yet in church they sit in the pews like zombies.

Many Christians have begun to realize that emotion is lacking in their spiritual lives. They sense that their omission is robbing them of two things: a full faith life and a well-adjusted emotional life at home and work. Searching for what's missing, some leave their childhood faith and opt for evangelical churches where Sunday smiles are abundant. They join charismatic groups or attend African-American services. (As one black priest puts it, "We're not more spiritual. We're just more emotional." He's too humble to say that his congregation might be both.) Many searching Christians today even tune in to TV preachers whose theology doesn't match their own but who at least deliver sermons with emotion.

But too many others just sit quietly and unblinkingly, separated from their emotions as if they were total strangers. When did we learn to act like this? In the case of men, they were influenced by an ethos that says emotions are feminine. Men are taught from childhood that it's not macho to show feelings, especially not tender ones. It's okay to be angry, but a man who brings flowers to his wife for no reason, weeps out of sorrow when a friend dies, cries when his child takes a first step, or sighs at an artistic expression of beauty is highly suspect.

Ironically, boys sometimes learn this lesson from their mothers. Mothers can be just as adroit as fathers in teaching their sons not to cry when they're hurt (physically or emotionally), not to run around the house when they're joyous, and not to scream in exasperation when a computer game proves too difficult to master. Some of those lessons are intended to instruct boys in the proper expression of emotions; but the lessons easily evolve into prescriptions against the feelings themselves.

Many girls are also given the same instruction. When they are disappointed, ridiculed, or wrongly blamed, they are not supposed to react emotionally, which would be the natural reaction. Instead, they are often told, "Don't cry," "You'll get over it," and even, "I know how you feel." Such advice short-circuits their expressions of emotion, turning feelings into something shameful: "You don't want them to see you cry, do you?"

As boys grow into adults, their teachers, drill instructors, bosses, and other authority figures reinforce the message that men are tough and should be able to take it. Ironically, as women try to equalize their roles in society, one unfortunate consequence is that they are challenged to hide their emotions.

We all know people who won't show their emotions because they are seen as signs of weakness. Someone who celebrates a sunrise is "weird." A man who cries when he loses his job is a "namby-pamby." A woman who pounds her desk in anger is a "victim of PMS or menopause." Anyone who sings or whistles for joy is probably "on drugs." In this view, emotions do appear to be a weakness. To be intelligent is to be strong and powerful; to be emotional is not.

Then there are those who equate emotion with a loss of control. For example, hours after I saw the birth of my daughter and was the first person in the world to hold her, I swirled into my office filled with delight and began handing out candy bars. The looks that greeted me said: "Calm down. This is a place of business." My joy was too effusive for the workplace.

There have been moments recently in our American culture when the public expression of emotion has been interpreted as weakness. Recall Edmund Muskie, who, while campaigning for president, cried when he heard that his wife had been attacked. He was not elected! Picture actress Sally Field accepting her Oscar and exulting, "You like me. You really like me." She has been ridiculed ever since. Think about football coaches who are not supposed to be angry or jubilant when their teams win or lose. The TV cameras want them stoic and "controlled."

We have all been taught well by parents, teachers, and religious leaders to quell our emotions. But we do much of the quelling all by ourselves. Emotions reveal something about us and expose us to others. It's sometimes like being caught naked in a spotlight. No wonder we cover up, hiding our emotions to keep from showing too much of ourselves. Yet, it is even riskier for our mental and physical health to seal emotions inside us, letting them build up pressure until we express them in the wrong way and at the wrong time.

We also censor our emotions to avoid commitment. As Jesus showed us over and over, emotions lead to action. When these actions are the right ones, they attach us to the object causing our emotions. We become involved. Therefore, we sometimes convince ourselves that the way to stay uninvolved is to stop feeling. When that is not possible, we do the next worst thing: We stop expressing our emotions.

There is one more culprit that robs us of expressions of emotion: religion itself. Thanks to strains of Jansenism and Manichaeism, which have infected Christianity for centuries, emotion for some is synonymous with sin; it is also defined as passion. Passion is identified with sexuality, and sexuality is always sinful.

In such a view, anything to do with the body is evil. Since emotions are expressed physically and are influenced by chemicals and genes, they must be evil.

Throughout his life, however, Jesus demonstrated that emotions are normal, natural, and neutral. They are part and parcel of being human. To be his follower means anything but being glum and indifferent. In scripture God makes this very, very clear: "You are neither cold nor hot. Since you are lukewarm, I spit you out of my mouth."

Chapter Ten

Rediscovering
Our
Emotions

$\mathcal{W}$e can learn again to express our emotions if we have forgotten how and to make them more vibrant if they are fading. One way to begin is to reclaim our feelings and to express them freely. I offer here suggestions for ways to better express our emotions in our spiritual life. In other words, here are ten ways to reignite your Christian emotions.

1. This Sunday at Mass, share the Sign of Peace in one of three new ways: with a stranger, with more emotion than usual, or with new words. For some people, this means sharing a sign of peace, period. Too many Catholics refuse to offer this sign of reconciliation and community, deigning to shake hands with relatives only.

This weekend, make a complete, 180-degree turn and greet someone you don't know. Smile as you wish that person the Sign of Peace. Even think of something new to say, like "May Christ be with you" or "I'll pray for you this week." You might be surprised at the emotion you get in return. It might be the alarm and fright the apostles felt when Jesus wished them peace after his resurrection. More likely, however, you'll get a warm and friendly smile in exchange for yours.

2. Tomorrow, as you read the daily newspaper or watch the news on TV, let yourself be touched by something. Don't turn the page or flip the channel. Let it affect you, and get in touch with your own feelings. Then decide to do something about what you saw, something other than writing a check. Find some way to become personally involved in solving a problem or comforting someone in trouble. Be like Jesus, who saw strangers in need and responded to them.

3. Right now in your life, there is probably someone you haven't spoken to in a long time but for whom you still have feelings. Maybe there was a rift, but more likely, it's just because life has

gone on, you've been busy, and that person has drifted away. Get in touch with him or her tonight by phone, letter, or a personal visit. Tell the person how you feel.

The separation between you and a loved one might not be geographic, and it might not have been lengthy in terms of time. Perhaps it's just that you haven't told your spouse or children that you love them. Maybe you have never thanked your parents for all they did for you. It could be that a close friend doesn't know how much he or she means to you. Break the silence before the sun sets tomorrow.

4. If you have children, share with them some religious feeling you have. Are you happy when you pray? Does God's love for you fill you with joy? Are you overwhelmed with gratitude when you think about your sins being forgiven? Whatever the feelings, don't keep them a secret. Let your children know that your faith affects you emotionally.

Alternative idea: Read the Bible until you find a passage that moves you. Read that portion to your children, and tell them why it has meaning for you and what emotions it stirs.

5. Decide that you will no longer mumble hymns in church. From now on, you will sing, loudly and lustily—perhaps even badly if you can't carry a tune. Let your emotions show in your voice, just as you might in your car when you're all alone and the radio plays your favorite song. Just as you do when a birthday cake is brought out, candles blazing.

6. The next time you donate money to a charity, give until it hurts—literally. Instead of the usual amount you pledge, double or triple it. Give so much that you have to do without something you want. Instead of an automatic gift, give a sacrificial one. It may begin as a pain in the wallet, but it will soon evolve into something else: the warm feeling of self-denial. Don't be like the rich young

man who went away sad when Jesus asked him to give all that he had.

7. If you feel angry about some injustice in the world right now, express it. Don't ignore your anger; let it out. Take positive actions, but be sure to right the injustice, if only in some small way. Express your anger about racism, sexism, abortion, capital punishment, economic oppression, hypocrisy—and then act on it.

8. Put yourself among Christians who feel more free to express their faith emotionally. Attend a charismatic gathering, for example. There you will see people whose voices can't keep up with the joy they want to express, whose praying hands cannot be contained at their sides, whose love for one another mirrors their love for Christ. You might be swept up in their emotions. Even if you aren't, you will have an experience that inspires you to pump up the volume on your own spiritual expressions.

9. Tell someone you trust about something you fear. That person could be a friend, relative, confessor, counselor, doctor, or someone else you have confidence in. If you can't think of anyone, just tell God. Just speak about your fear; don't worry about confronting it. Explain what your fear is and why you think you have it. As you do, perhaps you will start to feel comforted or to see a way out. Even if you don't, you will feel better. A shared load weighs half as much.

10. Avoid an emotion—if you know you are unable to express it appropriately. My last suggestion might seem like a contradiction after the other nine. As already noted several times, emotions themselves are morally neutral. How we express them sometimes involves morality, if we express them inappropriately. Morality can also be involved if we place ourselves in situations that are going to arouse emotions we can't control. In old-fashioned terminology, this might have been called avoiding occasions

of sin. We should also avoid situations that arouse emotions we know we can't handle.

For example, if you know that speaking to a certain person always causes you to become angry, and you don't know how to handle that anger, what is the point of putting yourself in this situation? It sounds like a common-sense issue, but all of us sometimes place ourselves in circumstances that arouse emotions we can't handle.

When Jesus sent his apostles out to preach his message, he gave them this practical advice: "If you come to a town that doesn't listen to you, don't make yourself crazy. Leave. Don't even take the dust from their streets with you. You can't help the people there, and they certainly won't help you. So what's the sense of hanging around getting angry? Move on."

Think about someone or someplace or some situation that leads you to express emotions you shouldn't express. Promise yourself to stay away from those situations.

By doing these things, we can begin to restore our emotional balance. When we become emotionally balanced, we become more Christ-like. And like him, we will respond properly to our feelings. We will have learned responses that will put us in touch with ourselves, with others, and with him.

Scripture References

Chapter One: Jesus Got Exasperated

Ezra 9

Mark 8:14–21

Mark 11:12–14

Mark 14:32–42

Luke 2:41–52

Mark 8:11–13

Mark 9:17–29

Luke 7:31–32

Matthew 13:36–43

Chapter Two: Jesus Felt Pity

Matthew 14:13–14

Matthew 20:29–34

Luke 7:13

Matthew 15:32–39

Mark 6:34

Chapter Three: Jesus Got Angry

Matthew 21:12–14

Matthew 11:20–24

Mark 3:1–6

Matthew 23:13–36

Chapter Four: Jesus Felt Fear

Luke 22:44

Matthew 26:39

Mark 5:36

Matthew 6:25–34

Mathew 26:37

Mark 4:35–41

Luke 22:41–44

Chapter Five: Jesus Loved and Was Lovable

Matthew 22:34–40	Mark 9:37
Mark 10:16	Mark 1:31
Mark 1:41	Mark 5:41
Mark 6:56	Mark 7:34
Mark 8:22–26	John 13:4–5
John 13:23	John 11:32–44
Luke 19:41–44	Matthew 5

Chapter Six: Jesus Was Sentimental

Luke 24:53	John 15:11
John 16:20–22	John 19:25–27
John 11	Luke 16:19–31
Mark 6:31	Luke 22:15, 32
John 13:4–5	Matthew 28:20
Luke 13:34–35	Luke 13:18–21
Luke 15:4–10	John 21:9

Chapter Seven: Jesus Felt Passion

Matthew: 26:63	Matthew 13:9, 15, 43
Luke 24:42–43	Luke 24:25–26
Mark 16:14–16	Mark 14:48–49
Luke 22:51	John 18:10–11
Luke 22:61	Luke 23:33–34; 39–43
John 21:9–19	

Chapter Eight: Jesus Had Emotional Followers

1 John 3:5	John 1:41–42
Matthew 14:22–23	Mark 14:26–31; 66–72
Matthew 26:75	John 18:10–11
Matthew 16:21–23	Luke 9:28–36
Matthew 19:27	John 13:6–11
John 21	Acts 1–12
1 Peter 3:9, 14; 4:7	Luke 10:29–37

Chapter Nine: Emotions and Christians Today
Revelation 3:15–16

Chapter Ten: Rediscovering Our Emotions

Luke 24:36–37	Mark 7:24–30
Luke 15:21–24	John 17:1–2
Matthew 26:30	Matthew 19:21
Mark 3:5	Acts 2:1–4
Luke 22:41–44	Mark 6:11

Of Related Interest...

Healing Wounded Emotions
Overcoming Life's Hurts
Martin Padovani
Describes how our emotional and spiritual lives interact, and challenges readers to live fuller, more satisfying lives.
0-89622-333-7, 128 pp, $6.95 (order W-22)
Audiobook: Three 60-minute cassettes, $24.95 (order A-44)

Pursuing Wellness, Finding Spirituality
Richard J. Gilmartin
This probing and dynamic book examines how we can become "well" through an examination of the physical, psychological and spiritual nature of humans. Gilmartin addresses interpersonal relationships, coping with stress, dealing with emotions, overcoming shame, death, freedom, our ultimate aloneness, and the meaning of life.
0-89622-674-3, 208 pp, $12.95 (order M-62)

Healing Words from Jesus
Isaias Powers, C.P.
Using stories of real-life people, Father "Ike" treats in an eminently practical way the heartfelt topics that readers will recognize from their own life experiences: positive thinking, forgiveness, patience, discouragement, peace of mind, gratitude, success, personal relationships, moodiness, and others. With down-to-earth advice Father Powers helps readers "negate the negatives" so that they may grow in closer union with Jesus and allow his healing power to have its effect on their lives.
0-89622-682-4, 152 pp, $7.95 (order M-60)

Available at religious bookstores or from:
TWENTY-THIRD PUBLICATIONS
XXIII P.O. Box 180, Mystic, CT 06355
To order or request a free catalog of other quality books and video call
1-800-321-0411